EAGLE COUNTY
a graphic guidebook

ISBN 978-1-60402-000-7

Edition A

blurb.com

EAGLE COUNTY
a graphic guidebook

INDEX

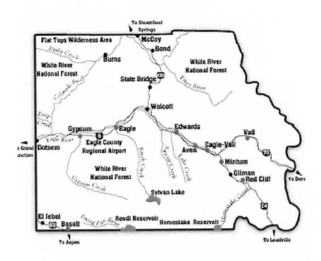

They come to ski Vail but
stay because of summer
(a local proverb)

I came to ski Vail but stayed because of everything else
that lies between Tennessee Pass and Glenwood Canyon.
What was here before the resorts with their manufactured
streetscapes and cosmetic facades? I found some answers
in the Eagle Public Library, on the information-filled
pages of the Internet and from helpful citizens who
remembered the past. I learned that the county takes its
name from the Eagle River that carved out a valley and
drew explorers along its pathway. Then came the
avaricious miners, homesteaders to plant its fertile
meadows and finally the mega resorts. These events left
landmarks and a vital history of a land that, no matter how
many want to change it, must always be called The Eagle
Valley.

Sherwood Stockwell   *July 1, 2010*

TIMELINE

4000 BC

In 1987, archaeologists discovered the Yarmony Pit House near State Bridge. The dig has yielded more than 4,600 artifacts from 4,000 BC.

2200 BC

The 2200 BC eruption of a volcano left a crater near the town of Dotsero.and cinder deposits that can be seen along Highway I-70.

1000 AD

Members of the Ute tribe came into the Western Slope to hunt and fish. By 1800 Ute Chief Ouray controlled a third of the region. It was said Utes didn't need to build pyramids like the Egyptians: they already had their mountains.

1859 AD

John H. Gregory discovered a gold lode in Colorado that prompted a rush of prospectors and pioneers. The Gregory became the first mining district in Colorado.

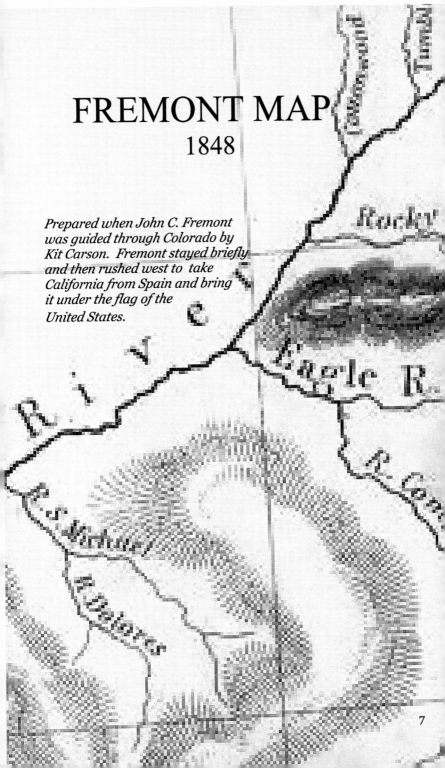

FREMONT MAP
1848

Prepared when John C. Fremont was guided through Colorado by Kit Carson. Fremont stayed briefly and then rushed west to take California from Spain and bring it under the flag of the United States.

EAGLE COUNTY

The Land

Eagle County was once just another slab of land under the Cretaceous Seaway, the ocean that split the continent of North America sometime between 65 and 145 million years ago. Then the seabed buckled up to form the Rocky Mountains, leaving volcanic craters and fish-like fossils imbedded in its folds that can be found today within the county boundaries.

The People

Artifacts discovered near Yarmony prove through age dating that humans occupied Eagle County during the ancient Miocene period. Eons later, Utes from the Great Plains came into what is now the county to gather food and game in its mountains and rivers. Despite rights guaranteed by treaty with the United States government, the Utes were forced off their lands as a result of an 1879 scuffle labeled the Meeker Massacre. The ensuing public outcry gave the United States Army an excuse to intern all the tribes in remote and barren reservations far away from the bountiful lands that became the county.

In the mid 1800's, Congress sent men to explore the great, unknown west. Soon, a rush of miners arrived to extract gold and silver from each side of the Continental Divide. The pioneers that followed created the Territory of Colorado and named its northwest quarter Summit County.

The Boundaries

In 1883, Eagle County was carved away from Summit with a meandering line that followed the crest of the Gore Range. Straight lines defined Eagle's three other boundaries. Rivers, however, define its geography. The Eagle River through its middle, the Colorado to the north, once known as the Grand River, and the Fryingpan to the Southwest were important to the mining, ranching and railroad industries and would later become magnets for the tourism that encouraged an expansion in the county from 7600 persons in 1970 to over 53,000 in 2009.

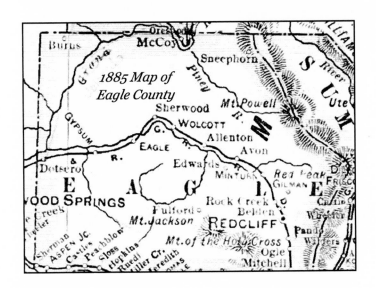

1885 Map of Eagle County

EAGLE RIVER

The River

The Eagle gave the county its name. It is the artery that pumps life into the county's land. Its tributaries are spread along its course, increasing the flow from its headwaters near Tennessee Pass to its confluence with the Colorado in Dotsero before the combined waters rush down through Glenwood Canyon.

The Utes named the river *Eagle* because the mainstream resembled the bird's long central feather and its tributaries the equal number of shorter side feathers. Today, the 70-mile long stream and its tributaries drain 944 square miles with a flow through Gypsum that averages 22,000 cubic feet per second.

Fremont

In 1845, Col. John C. Fremont was ordered to survey the Arkansa River. Instead, he came over Tennessee Pass and down the Eagle that he mistook to be the Piney. His party stopped near what is now Lake Creek. Fremont had to ford the river a number of times to avoid swamps and cliffs. The party's official cartographer, Charles Preuss, drew the first map to describe the river. His map on page 7 shows it as a wavy line intersecting The Grand, later to be renamed the Colorado. We can enjoy the beauty of the Eagle, but large cities like Denver and Las Vegas have more rights to its water, secured by decades of acquisition, counter claims and finally agreements after decades of litigation.

The Silver

In 1877 silver was discovered near the town of Leadville and miners set off in every direction to seek the lead carbonate that was the source of the precious metal. Their search led them over Tennessee Pass and then down along the river to what is now Redcliff. In 1880 the Eagle River Road Company used mule-drawn scrapers and boxes of dynamite to build a toll route beside the river and they added two bridges to ease the crossings. Soon, communities grew along the road to support the mining boom and produce enough population to form the new county.

The Railroad

The Denver & Rio Grande Railroad followed the river to shape the growth of the county. It gradually laid down rails to serve a dozen stops along the Eagle and most of the stops became the towns we know today. In the Southwest of the county, the Colorado Midland Railroad created new towns and both lines passed through places long forgotten with names like Ogle, Allenton, Rock Creek, Sloss Hopkins, Miller Creek and Mitchell.

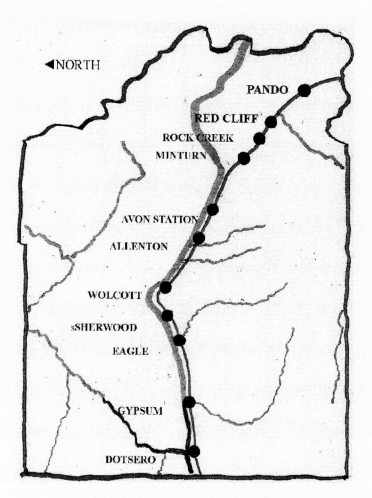

Route of the D & RG Railroad as it headed west and the new towns created as each track section was laid down.

THE WAY WEST

The Eagle River, that connects the county's east and west borders, was a natural route for the Utes who were the first on record to make a trail along its banks. The early hunters and then prospectors followed the Ute's trail. Once over the Continental Divide, it was the easiest pathway to reach the great Grand River. Soon farmers and shopkeepers came down the Eagle to settle along the way and open up the fertile lands for farming and ranching. The railroad barons used the route as they pushed in a frenzy to connect the bountiful silver mining communities. Today the paved highways continue to mark the way for those traveling between the county borders.

Past and Present

To describe the communities that make up Eagle County, this book follows the same path down the river that the Denver and Rio Grande Railroad took as it laid its rails from Leadville and created towns at each new extension. County history begins on the first stop the railroad made as it headed towards the Colorado River: a place called Pando.

PANDO

The Hollow

An 1887 photograph of the area called it Eagle Park. A railroad map of the same period, however, shows a stop between Leadville and Red Cliff at a station mysteriously named Pando. What's a Pando? In Latin p*ando* means *I spread* but in Portugese it means a *hollow* or *depression* in the land. Whether Italian or Portugese, it's easy to imagine a railroad employee spreading his arms out to a vast meadow that reminded him of similar places in his homeland.

Pando Flats

Pando is the point where two tributaries flow out of the mountains and meet to start the Eagle River. Before 1940, Pando Flats was an alpine meadow with a meandering stream running through it. Ponds created behind beaver dams produced winter ice that was cut and taken to Minturn for storage. During World War II, German prisoners were brought in to pack the large frozen blocks in sawdust for later use to refrigerate meats and vegetables.

World War II

After the 1941 attack on Pearl Harbor, skier Minot Dole convinced the War Department that they should prepare troops for alpine survival. This meant learning how to scale rocks, and, of course, mastering the use of skis on snow covered terrain.

Camp Hale

The Army searched for sites that would have easy access, suitable acreage that belonged to the federal government, venues for climbing and skiing and a snow cover that lasted more than 6 months. They narrowed the options down to West Yellowstone and a place named Pando. Pando was selected. Within an 8-month period, over 40,000 workers were involved in constructing a complete military post to house 16,000 soldiers and 3,900 pack animals.

The Army Engineers needed a level site for a typical military post. What they got were wetlands with a meandering Eagle River, so they channeled the stream and filled in an important wildlife habitat to create an environmental impact that may have equaled that caused when John C. Fremont, who camped nearby, killed the last buffalo on the Western Slope.

General Hale

The new post was named after Spanish American war veteran General Irving Hale who might not have relished having his name on a place with a 163 inch snowfall, where coal burning in thousands of stoves caused heavy air pollution and sometimes death.

10th Mountain Division

Camp Hale became the headquarters of the new 10th Mountain Division, whose 14,000 troops skied on nearby Cooper Hill, then the longest T-bar in the country. Sent abroad, the division seldom used their skis but they heroically breached the supposedly impregnable Gothic Line and secured the Po River Valley that was vital to the liberation of northern Italy.

Peacetime

Soldiers that skied nearby mountains stayed to develop them into now famous resorts. The alumni of Camp Hale opened Arapahoe Basin, revitalized the old mining town of Aspen, created a resort called Vail and spread out across the country to promote the fledgling sport. Ironically, the idea for Vail, that would forever change the tranquility of the Eagle River Valley, was spawned near the river's quiet headwaters. The county would never be the same. The Eagle was, in a sense, finally tamed.

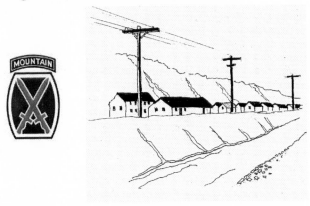

Although the buildings have been removed, the training grounds at Camp Hale are now historic landmarks.

RED CLIFF

*The 1890
Congegational
church on Main
Street*

Mining

Although Queen City and Jackass Flats were early names in the area, the surrounding red quartzite cliffs prompted Red Cliff, the first in a progression of mining camps and service towns that stepped down the river towards the west. In 1861, the new town had a scant 180 population. This expanded as miners intent on avoiding the crowds of Leadville found rich deposits of lead carbonate when they crossed Tennessee Pass and worked their way down the Eagle. They patronized the services offered by the citizens of Red Cliff (aka Redcliffe) and purchased timbers from its sawmill to shore up their tunnels.

Fort Arnett

After the Meeker Massacre in 1879, the overly concerned townsfolk were worried about attacks from the Utes and built a rough defense structure known as Fort Arnett on the large rock that stands today near Pine Street.

The D&RG

The Denver and Rio Grande Railroad extended from Leadville to Red Cliff in 1881 and everything along Monument Street shook with each dynamite blast as they cut the route through the rock cliffs. Red Cliff was the line's terminus until 1887.

The County Seat

In 1883, Red Cliff became the county seat of the newly formed Eagle County and decorum replaced its shoddy social structure. Things got so proper that two men who had killed each other in a brawl were refused burial in the town's new cemetery.

Winter

At elevation 8,750, winters were cold. In the 1880's the town was snowed in for 3 weeks and, running out of newsprint, the *Red Cliff Comet* was printed on wallpaper. The cold didn't stop Red Cliff's expansion that at its peak included 5 hotels, at least 2 saloons, a school and a post office.

The arched auto bridge, completed in 1941, spans the gorge where Turkey Creek joins the Eagle. It is listed on the National Register of Historic Places in Colorado.

Bridge History

The bridges over the Eagle were and are critical to travel. In 1897, 7 bridges burned between Red Cliff and Gold Park. Soon, steel or concrete structures replaced all the fragile timber spans. Now, many of these have also been replaced.

News

The first newspaper in Eagle, the *Eagle River Shaft,* started in 1875. It recorded the murder of Mike Gleason by Jack Perry who was caught heading for Leadville and hanged from a ladder on the D&RG water tower. The rung that held the rope was later stolen as a souvenir.

Shrine Pass

The road to Shrine Pass leads out of Red Cliff and follows Turkey Creek to higher elevations where one can view panoramas of the Sawatch, Gore and Ten Mile ranges. By mid-summer Shrine Pass has stands of beautiful wild flowers including Indian paintbrush and columbine, the Colorado State Flower.

Mount of the Holy Cross

First photographed in 1873, pictures by William H. Jackson of the snow cross inspired religious pilgrimages, the first sponsored by the Denver Post in 1912. Devotees claimed a nearby snow pile was an angel with hands raised in prayer. A small lake below was deemed a bowl of tears left by the angel's weeping over the crucifixion. A postage stamp issued in 1951 brought 2,000 to the commemorative ceremony.

GILMAN

High above the Eagle River, the abandoned town of Gilman is split by the tailings of the New Jersey Zinc Mine that once employed 450.

Clinton

The town of Gilman began as Clinton, but was soon renamed after a popular mine superintendent. It was built on a promontory 1,000 feet above a railroad stop called Belden. From Gilman, men lowered themselves down on buckets attached to a cable to work at mines with names like Silver Wave, Eagle Bird, Ground Hog and the Iron Mask.

Gilman Businesses

As the D&RG extended its rails and more mines were developed at Belden, the town of Gilman grew as a service center. The 1911 Colorado Business Directory listed the town's enterprising citizens. It would have been hard not to encounter a Buell in Gilman.

Bagge, Charles	Blacksmith
Buell , Emily	**Telephone Agent, Drugs, Postmistress, Cigars and Stationery**
Buell, W.N.	**Real Estate, Gilman Opera Liberty Bell Mine**
Clark , Mrs. J.	Music Teacher
Cleator, J.E.	Water Company
Forest, J.	Shoemaker
Forest, Mrs. J.	Forest Hotel Proprietor
Gritmaker, F.F.	Watchmaker
Spicer, Charles	Assayer
Vincent, W.F.	Real Estate
White, D.G.	Saloon

In 1879, the search for silver spread down the Eagle River and Judge Belden discovered lead carbonate and traces of silver a few miles below Red Cliff.

Belden

The judge built a mine and smelter near the river. Two years later the Denver and Rio Grande extended their tracks to serve the new mine at the Belden spur. In the 1920's The Empire Zinc Company tunneled into the cliffs above Belden. Their unique processing mill was located in a cavern carved inside the mountain between Gilman and the railroad.

Battle Mountain

Gilman is on the slopes of Battle Mountain where Utes and Arapahos fought over control of the land. Later, the New Jersey Zinc company that had consolidated many of the nearby mines fought its own battles for survival. Federal agencies finally closed down the mine in 1977 because heavy metals created by the operations were leaching into the Eagle River. The pollution killed schools of rainbow and brown trout and poisoned the water for downstream users.

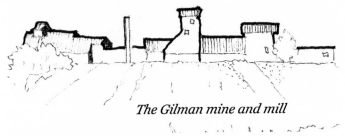

The Gilman mine and mill

Blue Sky Basin

Nearby Blue Sky Basin became a similar battleground when misguided activists, who fought expansion of the Vail Resort ski area, burned down Two Elk Lodge. Despite the mountain's battled history, a real estate developer hopes to turn Gilman into a private ski area, making it possibly become Eagle's Last Resort.

MINTURN

The Eagle flows by part of the old town that has been converted to retail shops and restaurants. In summer, it becomes the site of the popular Minturn Market.

Robert Bowne Minturn

In 1887 the Denver and Rio Grande pushed down to Kingston or Booco's Station, named after George C. Booco who had donated half of his ranch to establish a new town. The Booco name was soon changed to Minturn, a move probably proposed by Robert B. Minturn, Jr., an executive and director of the railroad. Minturn wanted to honor his father, Robert Bowne Minturn, who had large land holdings in the state of Virginia and was the owner of the *Flying Cloud,* the fastest Clipper Ship in the world. He was the first president of New York's Union League Club whose membership rules required *men of substance and established high position socially. A* confidant of many high government officials, Minturn was the prime promoter of New York's Central Park. He hoped the proposed open space would improve the city's culture, limit commercial growth and offer a healthy environment for its citizens.

The Community

The town named for Minturn hardly possessed any of his impressive credentials. The railroad that shut down in 1997 used its flat valley as a storage yard for freight cars serving the more affluent mining areas. It was the first community to be hit by the heavy metal pollution sent downstream from the New Jersey Zinc operations. Sidewalks didn't grace Minturn's Main street until 1917 and electricity came along 7 years later. Its hopes grew when nearby Meadow Mountain was selected as a venue for the 1976 Olympics, but it was deprived of the honor when Colorado refused to hold the international event.

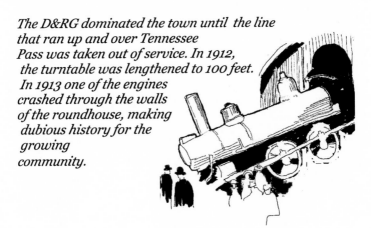

The D&RG dominated the town until the line that ran up and over Tennessee Pass was taken out of service. In 1912, the turntable was lengthened to 100 feet. In 1913 one of the engines crashed through the walls of the roundhouse, making dubious history for the growing community.

One of the first in the county, the Minturn Market opens every weekend in summer to provide a basketful of shops and kisoks that sell foods and arts and crafts.

The Minturn Market

Minturn saw its character and scale threatened by the expansion pressures of nearby Vail and Beaver Creek resorts. On the good side, residents of those resorts improved the town's economy as they elbowed out each other to touch and buy locally produced goods in the open-air Minturn Market.

The Saloon

The 1901 building was built by William H. Luby. His father, Hugh, started with the D&RG in Leadville and never left; but his children were very sucessful. William opened the saloon and became a judge and his brother Gene served as a county attorney.

Holy Toledo

The Unitarian Church with its Gothic window was built in 1917 at the corner of Main and Toledo. The structure now houses a clothing store aptly named Holy Toledo. Shoppers on Main Street shivered through the coldest winter on record in 1899 and trembled in the level 4, 1990 earthquake, one of 5 felt that week in Colorado.

AVON

Avondale

In the 1880's, Englishmen named Nottingham and Townsend settled along the Eagle River near the mouth of Beaver Creek. Some say that the area reminded them of England's Avon Valley, so they called it Avondale and then, simply, Avon. Railroad map makers misspelled it as *Avin* and later changed it to *Avon Station* or *Edwards PO*. The small town of Avon grew beside the river and one of its first shops can still be seen where it was moved to the Eagle County Museum in Eagle.

The Hahnewald barn has been restored and recycled for use by the local water and sanitation district.

Incorporation

Avon's agricultural role changed with the start of the new ski resort in Vail. Avon became a bedroom community for the resort's workers. When the resort owners decided to build a new ski village in the Beaver Creek Valley, many thought that both Avon and the new resort would be annexed to the existing Town of Vail. Instead, the independent Avon landowners filed for incorporation for their own separate community.

Roundabouts

After leaving highway I-70 a driver's first introduction to the town of Avon is a connector road whose 4 lanes and 5 roundabouts sprinkled with bronze horses enhance traffic flow but cut through and divide the village. The first roundabouts in the valley were built in Vail and the sceptics of the day have had to admit how well they work. The Avon roads are to serve the Beaver Creek resort where former farm buildings have been replaced with massive condominiums and the few restored log cabins of Bachelor Gulch are overwhelmed by the rustic envelope hiding a Ritz Carlton Hotel.

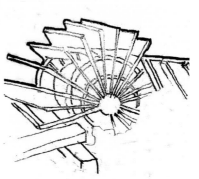

This wheel listed on the Colorado State Register of Historic Places once made electricity for the Nottingham Ranch. For $5.00 per month, it also powered the depot of the D&RG Railroad.

Iceberg Lettuce

Early Avon citizens grew hay and cattle to supply the bustling mining towns of Red Cliff and Gilman. By the 1920's head lettuce became the main agricultural product and the abundant, high-elevation sun allowed the farmers to produce 2 crops per year despite the short growing season.

*The crops that grew in this **Lettuce Capital of the World** were loaded onto freight cars and packed in frozen blocks from the Minturn ice house. When a form of rot hit the crop in 1923, the town lost its lettuce-backed title.*

Beaver Creek

Avon is the vehicular entry to nearby Beaver Creek where multi-storied condominiums vie with each other for splendor, their design features copied from farm buildings found in the more temperate foothills of Spain's Val d'Aran.

A single cabin of the original settlers along Beaver Creek is a featured landmark on a fairway of the Beaver Creek Golf Club.

Nearby Bachelor Gulch is named after single men Andersen, Berg, Mertz and Smith who inhabited the valley and survived by growing hay and trapping small game.

They defied state laws against shooting elk, claiming their catch was necessary in order to feed hungry miners up the line. They had a similar attitude when it came to distilling bootleg whiskey during the dry days of Prohibition.

EDWARDS

Berry Ranch

First called Berry Ranch in 1882, the crossroad community was renamed for or perhaps by Melvin Edwards, Colorado's then Postmaster and third Secretary of State.

In 1903, the town turned out to welcome Tom Fetch and Marius Krarup in their Packard Model F *Old Pacific*, the first auto to cross the United States by going through the Great Basin desert and over the high Rockies.

By 1911 the community of Edwards boasted a Justice of the Peace, a sawmill and a creamery. Such services have disappeared but many others can be found in mini-malls called Riverwalk, Edwards Corner and Edwards Village.

The Eagle River widens into slower waters. The river banks have been reconstructed to improve wildlife habitat.

New Development

The unincorporated town of Edwards grew larger as the expansion of Vail and Beaver Creek pushed populations down the Eagle Valley. Similar to neighboring Avon, Edwards grew before anyone could plan it as an integrated village. Unlike Minturn or Eagle, it lacks the unity of simple blocks laid out on compass points with storefronts lining the main streets. Instead, the old Berry Ranch has been divided into developments distinguished by their real estate prices: Arrowhead, Cordillera Valley, Single Tree, Homestead, Lake Creek Village, and a large mobile home park whose value as housing for Eagle Valley service workers far outweighs any higher land use.

Land Preservation

Most of Edward's subdivisions overlook or border the meadow where B& B has quarried sand and gravel to build the roads and structures of a growing Eagle County. The Vail Valley Foundation and the county purchased the scarred lands of the meadow to create a public preserve that may become the town's Central Park, a large enough focal point to tie together the separate community elements. The intent of the county is to replant the area with native trees, shrubs, grasses and wildflowers.

Eaton Ranch

72 acres of the Eaton family homestead lands have become the Eagle River Preserve that will provide Edwards with a central park and allow the rehabilitation of the riparian habitat along an important stretch of the river.

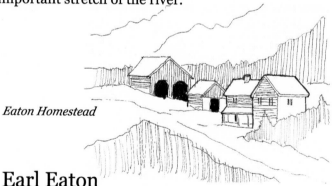

Eaton Homestead

Earl Eaton

A part-time prospector, Earl's greatest discovery was a no-name mountain he showed to Peter Seibert in 1962. At its base, they founded the new town of Vail. Eaton's reward, while others made millions from his find, was to have a circle in town renamed:

Eaton Plaza

Edwards Store

Built in 1920,the now demolished log structure was a
general store with the only gas pump in town. Despite
its name, the nearby Gas House didn't sell gas but it
began life in 1962 as a roadside stand nicknamed the
Awful Hamburgers.

Single Tree

Locals scoffed when a golf-club community was
proposed for the dry slopes north of I-70. Today, the
lush foliage around its homes belies its original
landmark, a single tree on an otherwise sparsely
planted hillside.

LAKE CREEK

*From Highway 6, the buildings of the
Brett Ranch hide the original log cabin
that is an imortant part of local history.*

Lake Creek

Lake Creek got its name from the Big Springs,
Thomas and Middle lakes that feed it. In 1845, John
C. Fremont camped at its junction with the Eagle,
noting it as *Williams Fishery,* where they made a
mysterious catch called a *Buffalo Fish,* that was
probably a whitefish. In 1879, Joseph Brett built his
log cabin nearby. Brett had migrated to the Leadville
mines when the Prussians overran his homeland in
Alsace-Lorraine. He soon moved on to the Eagle
Valley, forsaking the lure of a silver strike for the less
risky job of raising crops to feed the miners.

The Frenchman's

Brett's Ranch was better known as *The Frenchman's* where people as famous as railway magnate Jay Gould came to hunt elk and bear, fish for trout and lose fortunes at Brett's card tables that were housed in a nearby tent. His house rules were simple:

***No Rowdiness, No Hot Water
and Wash Up at the Trough.***

Lake Creek School

Teaching

In 1900, the Lake Creek School was a one room classroom taught by Georgia Devereux whose student body of 24 included 5 Cunninghams, 4 Wellingtons and 2 Bretts. Based on their number of children, Messrs. Cunningham and Brett could always outvote board member Wellington who seldom had a chance to prevail. As compensation for her teaching, the board offered Georgia a bonus of $10.00 per month if she'd agree to do the janitoring.

SQUAW CREEK

*The red schoolhouse
still stands today on
Squaw Creek Road
on the way into
Cordillera.*

Bearcat Bearden

Ellis *Bearcat* Bearden, lived near Squaw Creek in a
log cabin that his family had homesteaded since 1913.
Nicknamed during his boxing days, Bearcat resisted
takeover attempts by the gated community called
Cordillera. Money meant little to Bearcat. Eager to
buy his acreage, Cordillera developers invited him to a
posh lunch and proposed a generous price. Bearcat, in
his Oshkosh overalls, simply shook his head to their
offer, pushed back his plate and pocketed a slice of
turkey to save for dinner.

*Bearden frustrated Cordillera residents by stopping his hay truck
in the middle of the road and refusing to move until they helped
him pitch off the load to feed his cows.*

Cordillera

The name Cordillera is literally translated from Spanish as the *little cord*, but it's been changed over time to describe the geography between two mountain chains. Built on the ridge tops that overlook Squaw Creek, the 7,000 acre subdivision on much of what was the Fenno Ranch boasts 4 golf courses, an equestrian center, post office and prominent lodge/hotel. The lodge received national recognition with a professional basketball star named Kobe Bryant whose escapades brought on lawsuits and an influx of media traffic that tied up the county seat at Eagle for a week.

Stagecoach Route

At Squaw Creek's mouth, the route for the stagecoach turned away from the Eagle's steep canyon walls to follow the creek, climb up Penny Gulch to stop at the Howe's spring that Bearcat Bearden said was so cold that stage riders would keel over. Those that survived rode over the ridge to Brush Creek and Eagle.

Shepards' Wagons

WOLCOTT

A faded sign on the old boathouse dubbed it as the Wolcott Yacht Club. A popular restaurant across the street was inspired to borrow the same name.

Russells

The place was first named Russells,and also possibly misprinted as *Bussels,* after William Russell. Russell built a sawmill there to cut ties for the railroad that was pushing west; but when the tracks got to Glenwood Springs, local sawmills beat out Russell's prices. The mill was shut down and in 1889 the D&RG depot was renamed after U.S. Senator Edward O. Wolcott, possibly because the senator was a great orator, an advocate for coinage of silver and, not incidentally, an attorney for the D&RG.

Agriculture soon replaced timber as Wolcott's major economy. Farmers diverted the waters of the nearby Eagle River to irrigate the valley meadows and ranchers grazed their herds in the surrounding countryside before corraling them in stockyards near the Wolcott Hamlet.

The Railroad

As Eagle County's herds increased to the 10,000 mark, Wolcott became a major stop on the Denver & Rio Grande. At one time, the railroad loaded over 2,000 cattle cars a year here and sent them east to the slaughter houses. Tens of thousands of dollars in gold from their sales had to be shipped elsewhere because Wolcott lacked a bank for safekeeping.

Booco Mountain

William Booco was the son of George G. Booco, whose gift of land started the town of Minturn. William owned a large ranch in Wolcott and his name is memorialized on a nearby mountain. His grandfather came to America with Lafayette, adding French to Wolcott's ethnic diversity that included Scotch, Irish, Swedes, Italians and the county's only African-American who was known as Negro Rose.

Covered Bridge to Eagle Springs

Koprivnikar Barn

This 1911 structure, one of the few along the river in Wolcott, sits near the 18th hole of the Eagle Springs Golf Club.

Old Schoolhouse

The belfry tower identifies what once housed the educational facilities when Wolcott was a burdgeoning community. The abandoned building sits behind a wooden fence near the Gallegos stone yards and the D&RG railroad tracks.

The Jouflas Ranches

Most of Wolcott's land is divided between two Jouflas families whose predecessor owned grazing rights that extended as far east as what is now Vail. Some of the land was sold off to become Red Sky Ranch and much of the remaining land, particularly that on the valley floor, is being planned for development.

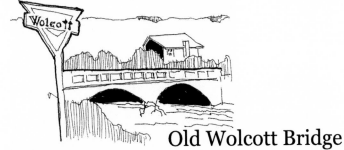

Old Wolcott Bridge

In 1890,Herwick built the first bridge over the Eagle at Wolcott. It was replaced in 1910 by a double concrete span built by Pueblo Bridge Co. One of the few landmarks in the county, it too was destroyed in 2006 to make way for a standard precast replacement.

The Hamlet

The Wolcott Hamlet contains the old Wolcott Inn and the Wolcott Yacht Club, 2 residences, a restaurant that replaced the old post office and gas station. At one time the village boasted 3 livery stables, a blacksmith, 2 hotels and a requisite number of saloons. Today, a few residences plus a 1924 log cabin moved down from Bellyache Ridge are sheltered by a large stand of willow trees.

From the abandoned railroad tracks, one looks east to the landmark escarpment on the north and Bellyache Ridge to the south.

Bellyache Ridge

In Wolcott the land south of Highway I-70 slopes up to form Bellyache Ridge. Roads with the name *Bellyache* climb up the ridge from 3 different directions. Hang gliders launch from its cliffs and deer and elk abound. Some claim the Ute Indians named it after getting sick from drinking alkali water from the creeks and ponds. Others claim it was an after effect of a bumpy stage coach ride to the top.

Viewed from the Hamlet, Castle Peak is distin-guished by its crenelated top, but from Bellyache Ridge it looks more like a pyramid in the afternoon shadows.

Road to Steamboat

In 1886, workers from Wolcott cut a roadway that is now Highway 131 from the Hamlet to the old town of Steamboat Springs. The road not only served to bring cattle down to Wolcott's stockyards but it was the only route north from the railroad for transporting materials and mail between the two points.

SHERWOOD

A spot on the map

An 1895 map of the Denver and Rio Grande Railroad shows all the stops on their line through Eagle County. Lost to history are places named Mitchell, Rock Creek, Allenton and a spot on the map between Eagle and Wolcott called Sherwood. The only sign left of the latter is an irrigation channel called Sherwood Ditch and the arched concrete bridge that connected the railroad stop with the roadway on the south.

The Bridge

The 2-span concrete bridge at Sherwood resembles the old bridge in Wolcott and may have been built by the same engineer whose name was Daniel B. Luten. Luten held over 30 patents for reinforced concrete arch bridges and claimed the design of more than 12,000 of them during his lifetime.

Rupert M. Sherwood

Nearby ranchlands were first settled in 1890 by a man named Rupert M. Sherwood. Such properties were typically acquired under terms of a law signed by Abraham Lincoln called the Homestead Act. To promote expansion of the west, a homesteader received title to 160 acres if he'd farmed the land for 5 years and built a house with minimum outside dimensions of 12 by 14 feet.

From the Sherwood cliffs, a horse-drawn drum and pulley system dropped red sandstone to the railroad down below. The stone was used on buildings like the Brown Palace in Denver.

The Discovery

In 1904, locals were shocked by the discovery of a decomposed body in Sherwood, identified by letters of recommendation in his pocket as that of O.E. Frederichsen. After a separation from his wife and children, he'd become a drifter and was apparently killed by a large boulder set loose from the cliffs above. His obituary described him as:

> *A competent man in his line when sober but a victim of strong drink*

EAGLE

Near this steel bridge, a 1909 train collision killed 21 people including two, 5-person families. An accident in 1943 overturned the engine and freight cars but spared those carrying army troops on their way to the Pacific.

The name

Brush, Castle, Eagle River Crossing, Rio Aquila and MacDonald were names once given to the town of Eagle. Railroad maps called it Rio Aquila, one of the few recognitions of the Spanish influence in the county, but the name Castle prevailed. In 1893, owner B. Clark Wheeler sold Castle to A.A. MacDonald, a miner that went broke trying to hit a silver lode by driving a mine shaft into Battle Mountain. Unable to pay his crew, he offered double wages if they kept going until they hit paydirt. His gamble was successful and in 1895 MacDonald celebrated by legally vacating the name Castle and dedicating the new town to himself.

Finally Eagle

Despite A.A. MacDonald's sponsoring a road to Burns to entice Colorado River travelers from the Wolcott route, the town of MacDonald failed to blossom. Its owner defaulted and the town was resold for $210.42 in back taxes. A year later, the town officially became Eagle.

The County Seat

The town could boast the first telephone in the county via the Parkison line to Glenwood Springs and, by 1912, electric street lighting. Getting to be the county seat wasn't that easy. Successive votes in 1895, 1904 and 1912 retained the title for Red Cliff. The vote shifted in favor of Eagle in 1920 and by 1932 the commissioners had moved the County Court out of the Brush Creek Saloon into a new 3-story concrete box designed in the Art Deco style .

The Character

When asked, "What elements of Eagle's character should be preserved?" most residents wanted to keep the small-town, *Western* feeling of the close-knit community. The town retained this character for years by voting down repeated proposals for a new ski resort called Adam's Rib; but Eagle's attraction as an alternative to the high-priced life in Vail created other new developments whose daily traffic sometimes chokes the once quiet downtown streets.

Eagle County Historical Society

Located near the County Fairgrounds at Chambers Park, the museum is housed in a barn moved from Castle Peak Dairy to make way for I-70. Near the barn are a caboose from the D&RG and an historic log cabin moved here that once was Avon's store.

201 Broadway

The 1887 Duncan House Hotel and Saloon was converted in 1893 to the Eagle Valley Bank. After a fire, it was rebuilt in 1897 to house a butcher shop and barber and later Cramp's Cash Store. In 1908 it became the First Bank of Eagle.

223/225 Broadway

In 1904 the Dice brothers built the second brick building in Eagle. Beside the Pony Resort Saloon and a pool hall, an addition held the Silver Eagle barbershop and bath (25 cents per use). After 1909 the building occupants included a drug store, soda fountain, Enterprise newspaper offices and the US Post Office.

301 Broadway

The Eagle Pharmacy sign proudly announces it as the *Almost Everything Store.* It has carried close to anything ever requested by customers in Eagle, from the latest prescription drugs and an hibachi to a canoe that once hung from the store ceiling .

Nogal Store and Hotel

In 1888, Charles F.Nogal, Postmaster at what was then called Castle, built a store and added tents to house and feed workers for 25 cents per night. Three years late he erected a hotel (shown left, below) that boasted 8 bedrooms and a total capacity of 26, if you didn't mind sharing space.

Ping Hotel

In 1923, Nogal sold his property to the Pings who added a gas pump and two outbuildings along Capitol Street. The two small structures were once connected by a false front bearing a sign proudly identifying them as the *Ping Cottages*.

Methodist Church

The steeple of the 1900 church and parsonage is beyond the hotel cottages. It has served for a century as a place of worship and gathering area for civic events.

Nogal and Ping Hotel with Methodist Church beyond

The historic barns
served the cattle
loafing yards of the
original ranch.

Eagle Ranch

The village spirit of old Eagle has been copied in Eagle Ranch where residents can sit on Midwestern style verandas and easily walk tfrom there to the store. Eagle Ranch is blessed with views of the 14,000 foot peaks of the *Sawatch* range,the name derived from the Ute *Saguache*, meaning *Water at the Blue Earth.*

A logo of the Polar Star mine is
now on a 10th Mountain hut
door. At one time Fulford was
named after the mine and it
was known as Polar City.

Fulford

The town of Eagle grew when silver ore was found in nearby Fulford, a town named after a Red Cliff marshall who died in a snow slide. Mines like Anthony and Cleopatra, Old Maid and Butterfly had great names but short lives. Today's attractions are limited to the Mayfield Cave carved by nature out of the limestone mountainside.

GYPSUM

White plumes rising across the Eagle River identify the American Gypsum plant for drivers along I-70. Nearby a series of ponds ,left when material was excavated for the highway, are now state wildlife areas.

1884

By 1884 there were 31 ranches in the Gypsum Valley and 4 years later the new community of Gypsum had a population of 50 and boasted a blacksmith, general store, saloon, restaurant, hardware store and livery stable. This was enough to convince the D&RG to push its line from Leadville to the growing town named after a mineral. The new railroad made it easier for Gypsum farmers and ranchers to sell their products in the more populous areas around the county seat of Red Cliff.

The Mineral

While other mining towns ran out of precious metals a century ago, Gypsum still has an abundant supply of the mineral that is used to produce sheetrock in the largest manufacturing facility in Eagle County. Gypsum is a sedimentary material that was formed under the sea that once covered Colorado. It is found in such diverse places as the sands of Great Sands National Park, board chalk used in schools and even the junk food *Twinkies.* Gypsum makes it possible for 120 employees of the American Gypsum plant to produce 56 million square meters of wallboard a year, enough to build over 75,000 homes.

The collapsed old bridge was once a main entrance to Gypsum. It repeats the design of the 2-arch bridges that crossed the Eagle at Sherwood and Wolcott.

President Roosevelt

In 1905 Gypsum made headline news when President Theodore Roosevelt hired local guide Jake Borah. Jake's customers during the previous year had killed 43 bears and 34 mountain lions, but deer and elk were not on the list. Killing them was forbidden by a statewide ban to reduce their wholesale slaughter by hunters that sold the meat to wealthy miners. Realizing the importance of his visit, however, the governor issued a special permit to the president so he could kill any kind of animal. Roosevelt sensed the political ramifications and refused to use the permit, stating that it would be violating the game laws of Colorado. Instead, Roosevelt 's party bagged 10 bears and 2 bobcats.

Red Soil Potatoes were a major product from Gypsum's sandy soils up to the 1960's when the market was taken away by farmers in Maine and Idaho.

POTATOES

GROWN & PACKED BY

SLAUGHTER RANCH

GYPSUM, COLORADO 81637

First Evangelical Lutheran Church

Dates for building this example of Gothic Revival Architecture ran from 1875 to 1899. The church is listed on the National Register of Historic Places. Stained glass arched windows date from the original construction.

First Street

A 3-story building from the 1900's rermains on the west side of First Street as an historic reminder of the once bustling row of lodgings and storefronts. Nearby, Frank Doll built the first flour mill in town.

DOTSERO

Built in 1934, this is one of the few remaining Parker steel truss bridges in Eagle County. The green painted structure is near the spot where the first bridge crossed the Colorado River in 1887. Similar steel truss bridges were built near Sherwood and on Highway 6 above the town of Eagle. The 150-foot clear span in Dotsero and the shorter steel span in Eagle are both listed on the National Historic Register.

The confluence

The Eagle River joins the Colorado and the D&RG splits into two branch lines near a place called Dotsero. This is the confluence for both water and rails before they dash down between the high rock walls of Glenwood Canyon. When silver was discovered in the nearby Flatops, optomistic miners rushed up through the canyon only to find that early snowstorms would maroon over 1000 of them in Dotsero, making it temporarily the second largest settlement in the county after Redcliff.

The Name

Dotsero? Early settlers claimed it was the name of an Indian chief's daughter, but scholars note that there is no equivalent for a *D* in the Ute alphabet. Some said Dotsero simply described the midpoint between the Rockies and the Pacific. The name's most likely source, however, was the 1877 geological survey map by Ferdinand Hayden who designated the site as Dot Zero or the starting point of the survey. The name was repeated on an 1885 engineering map to set the takeoff point for the railroad cutoff that would run along the Colorado and through the Moffat Tunnel to shorten the trip from Salt Lake to Denver by 150 miles. The end of the cutoff was amusingly labeled Orestod ,which is Dotsero spelled backwards

Denver & Rio Grande

When the railroad reached Dotsero, the county was finally bound together with steel rails in the same way that it was tied together by the waters of the Eagle River. The county would not have grown so rapidly without the rails and the rails wouldn't have grown so easily without the river route to follow. Despite its historic importance, rail traffic decreased between Dotsero and Red Cliff until the line was shut down in 1997. It is still maintained as an emergency alternative to the Moffat Tunnel route, although many towns, a golf course and real estate developers would like to use the right of way themselves.

Charlie ruled the Utes that once occupied Dotsero. His real name was Sapiah.
Born about 1840, he eventually succeeded Chief Ouray as the Utes' official treaty negotiator.

Buckskin Charlie

Of necessity he learned the white man's rules and mastered the white man's tongue, but Charlie only embraced white culture to the extent that it helped the Utes preserve their own.

Utes left their messages to others by scratching pictures into the rock walls of a cave near Sweetwater Lake.

Ute Pictographics

The original Ute trail followed the Eagle to Dotsero where branches led to the Frying Pan River and the Flatops. The trail over the Flatops led up Sweetwater Creek to Sweetwater Lake. The pictographs are found on nearby private land just over the border in Garfield County. Guides from the lodge on the lake run tours to the caves.

Dotsero Volcano

Although the name Dotsero is typically identified with the railroad,there are similar sounding Ute words that denote a *unique or new event*. The *unique event* could have been the eruption of the Dotsero Volcano tin 2200 BC that created a basaltic lava flow that spread to the south and diverted the Eagle River to the other side of the valley. The volcanic ash from the flow is visible on each side of Highway I-70. For years the main industry of Dotsero was manufacturing cinder blocks from the ash.

A *marr* or shallow depression marks the spot of the eruption. The USGS rates the volcano as only a moderate threat that is not likely to reoccur in a human lifetime.

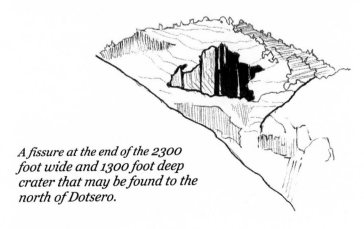

A fissure at the end of the 2300 foot wide and 1300 foot deep crater that may be found to the north of Dotsero.

Colorado River Road

Peterson Flats

The cabin on the Colorado River Road was built in 1885 and occupied in the early 1900's by Charley Peterson. It holds a still unsolved mystery: Charley was murdered and his body was found under a pile of brush. The only clue left was a dining table set for three, indicating that Peterson and his assailants had eaten together before the crime. The cabin was ransacked but the killers missed $104.20 hidden in the cabin wall. The Homestead land is being developed as the site of Roundup River Ranch. It is a Hole in the Wall retreat whose program was started by Paul Newman where children with serious illnesses, in his words, could:

> ***sit back, relax, raise a little***
> ***hell and just be kids.***

Burns

The name came from trapper Jack Burns. The community was large enough to deserve a post office in 1895. Despite the fact that nature never salted the upper half of the county with precious metals, the area grew when the D&RG built the cutoff from Dotsero to Orestod. Burns Hole on the Colorado River Road became a stockyard where ranchers could hold their cattle for shipment east on the railroad. The yards were built in exchange for the right of way needed by the railroad to go through the Benton Land and Livestock Company. Frank Benton purchased the land in 1907 from a man from Chicago named Kenner who came to the Burns area each summer in the 1890's. The place was known as *Thirteen* because of the 13 log cabins that Kenner built.

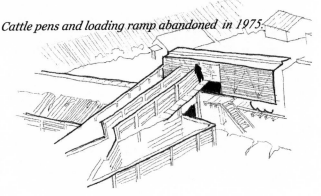

Cattle pens and loading ramp abandoned in 1975.

Highway 131

4-Eagle Ranch

The north county grew when the road was built from Wolcott to Steamboat Springs. Now called Highway 131, the road rises out of Wolcott on a shoulder of Bocco Mountain and enters the long valley that contains the 4-Eagle Ranch with its homesteader cabins that date back to the 1800's. The ranch that is now used for special events is threatened for possible future destruction if the valley becomes flooded for a reservoir.

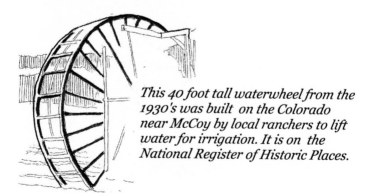

This 40 foot tall waterwheel from the 1930's was built on the Colorado near McCoy by local ranchers to lift water for irrigation. It is on the National Register of Historic Places.

McCoy

In 1890 travelers crossed the Colorado using *Old Daddy* McCoy's ferry. The stage they used cost $7.00 for the trip from Wolcott to Steamboat Springs. They might have stopped at the McCoy Hotel, built where the road crossed Rock Creek. The ferry was replaced and the hotel lost patrons when the state built the new bridge upstream. A trail from McCoy follows Rock Creek to the Cinder Pit, site of lava deposits similar to those in Dotsero. The railroad here has sidings called Volcano and Crater, where evidence of more cinders verifies ancient volcanic activity.

The Rock Creek valley provided good land for raising hay that was stored in barns near the big bend on Highway 131.

STATE BRIDGE

The State Bridge

In 1891 the legislature of the young state appropriated $5,190 for construction of a bridge to be located on the river 8 miles above McCoy. The double span Howe Truss structure was built out of logs fastened with wood pegs and it was given the name of State Bridge.

The view above no longer exists. The log bridge was replaced by a modern concrete span and the nearby lodge was destroyed by a tragic fire after its 1985 listing in the National Register.

Events

State Bridge today is a venue for summer music events and is a popular terminal for river float trips. Over 25 trains a day pass by the site, most of them carrying coal from the Craig mines.

The Lodge

A small stage coach depot was built near the new bridge on an unworked mining claim at the foot of Yarmony. The mountain was named after a famous chief of the Utes that inhabited the area. The depot grew into the two-story State Bridge Lodge that had its greatest publicity day when President Theodore Roosevelt stayed in cabin 3 on his way to hunting elk in the Flat Top Mountains.

Old Yarmony Bridge

Yarmony

The Yarmony bridge spanned the Colorado at a point between Radium and State Bridge. In 1894 a post office opened to serve the small community. Nearby, archaeologists discovered stone tools in what is called the Yarmony Pit House. The prehistoric camp and habitation dates to the Mount Albion Complex period over 6000 years ago. Tests show that temperatures then were warmer than today. The Pit house is listed on the National Register as an Archaic Period Architectural site.

SOUTHWEST

A Separate World

Although separated from the rest of the county by Red Table and Basalt mountains, the county's southwest includes the lower Frying Pan River and its confluence with the nearby Roaring Fork. The latter's valley was the logical route for the Colorado Midland Railroad that created new communities as it extended service from Glenwood Springs to the important new mining town of Aspen.

El Jebel

El Jebel began life as a railroad stop called Sherman. The name was change to the Arabic word for *mountain* by the ranch owner who was an avid member of the El Jabel Masonic temple in Denver. In 1883 a road was built from El Jebel to Meredith, east of the present Reudi reservoir. To get from El Jebel to the important Eagle County town of Basalt, one must pass by a place called Emma.

Kilns in nearby Pitkin County at Thomasville provided lime between 1889 and 1908 for mortar and for processing different metals.

Emma

By the grace of the cartographer's straight line, Emma happens to be pushed by .004 degrees into Gilpin County; but a view of it's ruins can't be missed. The D&RG and the Colorado Midland Railway both passed through the town of Emma where brickmaker J. M. Barnes supplied products to residents like Postmaster Charles Mather, whose 19th century Queen Anne Victorian house stands nearby.

Remains of Mather's Mercantile buildings can be seen on the north side of highway 82, betweenBasalt and El Jebel. Pitkin County plans to preserve them.

Ghost Towns

Places like Castles, Peachblow, Missouri Heights and Thomasville that grew up along the Frying Pan and the CMRR have nearly disappeared. In the county north of Thomasville, the 41 log buildings of the Woods Lake Resort are listed on the National Register, although the resort closed in 1933.

BASALT

The Town

At one time the Colorado Midland Railroad ran down the center of town and then on to the St. Louis and Colorado Smelter in Thomasville. The railroad named the stop Frying Pan Junction but in 1887 changed it to Basalt after nearby Basalt Mountain.

History

Historic structures in Basalt include the 1888 Lutheran church, the abandoned steel truss bridge to Emma and the Emery Arbaney Barn, built in the early 1900's. Arbaney was one of the many immigrants from Aosta, Italy and nearby villages in Switzerland that came to Basalt to operate charcoal ovens. When the charcoal demand ran out the town suffered;but, close to Aspen and Glenwood Springs, the town has now become a popular residential community.

The old railroad station on the left now houses a bank. The brick building was once a hotel and the building next door was a garage with a Conoco gasoline sign gracing its false front.

Charcoal

Unlike the silver carbonates, basalt had little value except as ballast to hold railroad ties. The town provided a more important product than basalt: charcoal. Made from the large nearby stands of pinion pine, the charcoal was used to operate the smelters in Aspen and Leadville. Charcoal was shipped out on the Colorado Midland line until coal was discovered in nearby Carbondale. The coke made from coal replaced charcoal in the smelters and Basalt's ovens became a local historic landmark.

Beehive Ovens

In 188,27 ovens, 25-feet in diameter and 25-feet high, were built near the confluence of the Frying Pan and Roaring Fork rivers. Known as the Frying Pan Kilns, they were active until coke replaced charcoal in the Aspen and Leadville smelters.

Beehive ovens

VAIL

The early tower and covered bridge landmarks are now dwarfed by large hotels and condominium complexes.

The Highway

Almost a century after the silver rush spawned towns along the Eagle, a different phenomena created the county's economic driving force. Many books describe how Earl Eaton led Pete Seibert to the Back Bowls of what is now called Vail Mountain. They named the mountain and town at its base to honor the highway engineer that created the route over the Gore Range. Without the highway connecting it to the outside world, there would probably have been no Vail.

The Resort

At the bottom of the new Vail Pass, Eaton and Seibert identified large ranch holdings that would provide the necessary land to build a ski base. Then, they sought out wealthy backers willing to risk the funds to finance the project. This would be the first large community that wasn't located on the Eagle River but on a tributary called Gore Creek.

The fledgling ski area that began in 1963 has 5000 acres of terrain to make it the largest in the country. The publicly traded corporation now owns half a dozen major resorts and operates as many hotels.

Vail Planning

At a local meeting, architect Fitzhugh Scott, one of the earliest residents of Vail, was asked to describe the city planning process that went into laying out the famous mountain village and its picturesque Bridge Street.

"It was simple," he said. "I had a client that wanted to build a lodge next to the mountain and Fritz Benedict had a client that wanted to build a motel on the highway. Bridge Street was the dirt path between the two."

The Gore Name

The creek, the range of peaks, and half a dozen other places that also bear the name, memorialize another sort of risk-taker named Sir St. George Gore. Gore, wrongly dubbed with the title of a Lord, has been touted as an ardent sportsman who spent two grueling years hunting in the wilds of the west.

Actually, the very wealthy Irish baronet toured the Rocky Mountains with a retinue that included his own valet, a silk tent, steel bathtub, 100 horses, 75 rifles, 50 hounds and 250 gallons of *Trade Whiskey,* a blend of 180 proof grain alcohol, pepper and tobacco supposedly helpful in making bargains with the Indians. With these provisions and Jim Bridger as a guide, Lord Gore managed to kill 2500 buffalo, 1,600 elk and 150 bears just for sport. The adventure ended ingloriously when a trader for the American Fur Company refused to pay what Gore thought was a fair price for all his fancy equipment. Annoyed, Gore started a bonfire and most of his trophies and gear went up in smoke.

Colorado Ski Museum

The famous slopes at Vail have welcomed many top skiers since 1962. Over the years, downhill techniques have changed and the history of the the transition is shown in the costumes and equipment on view at the Colorado Ski Museum in the Vail Transportation Center.

Katsos Cabin

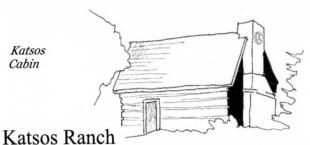

Katsos Ranch

The Katsos cabin was on one of the ranches that Vail founders bought for an average price of $150 per acre. To avoid paying inflated land costs, agents of the founders purchased the land under the guise of using it as a site for a rod and gun club.

The New Vail

In a brief half century, Vail has grown to an estimated 5,000 permanent and 5,000 part time residents. It's switched much of its architecture from a modernized Swiss to an interpreted Bavarian that now dominates much of the landscape along I-70.

Acknowlegements

The story of *EAGLE COUNTY* is told here with images and a related text that may not be historically precise because much of the information is in the form of personal writings of individuals that don't always agree. The most comprehensive sources reviewed were *Early Days on the Eagle* by Macdonald Knight, 1965, and a 1940 collection of essays by Eagle County school children found with help from historian Jaci Spuhler of the Eagle Valley Library District.

Many of the ink sketches were derived from watercolor paintings in an earlier book called *EAGLE* that is available from the same publisher or through The Bookworm, Edwards. The photographic archives of both the Eagle Valley Library District and the Eagle County Historical Society also provided background material for the sketches.

Also by the Author

Novels
Stealing Santa Rita
Threads to Untangle
Las Arenas

Monographs
When the Lions Come
Reel Tales
Eagle
Portfolio